BEYOND

FARRAR

STRAUS

GIROUX

NEW YORK

JOHN KOETHE

Farrar, Straus and Giroux
120 Broadway, New York 10271

Published in 2022 by Farrar, Straus and Giroux
First paperback edition, 2023

Grateful acknowledgment is made for permission to reprint excerpts
from "Dockery and Son" and "Sad Steps" from *The Complete
Poems of Philip Larkin* by Philip Larkin, edited by Archie Burnett.
Copyright © 2012 by The Estate of Philip Larkin. Reprinted by
permission of Faber and Faber Ltd. and Farrar, Straus and Giroux.

The Library of Congress has cataloged the hardcover edition as follows:
Names: Koethe, John, 1945– author.
Title: Beyond belief : poems / John Koethe.
Description: First edition. | New York : Farrar, Straus and Giroux, 2022. |
Identifiers: LCCN 2022021889 | ISBN 9780374604332 (hardcover)
Subjects: LCGFT: Poetry.
Classification: LCC PS3561.035 B49 2022 | DDC 811/.54—dc23/eng/20220510
LC record available at https://lccn.loc.gov/2022021889

Paperback ISBN: 978-0-374-60786-9

Designed by Crisis

Our books may be purchased in bulk for promotional, educational, or
business use. Please contact your local bookseller or the Macmillan Corporate
and Premium Sales Department at 1-800-221-7945, extension 5442,
or by email at MacmillanSpecialMarkets@macmillan.com.

www.fsgbooks.com
www.twitter.com/fsgbooks
www.facebook.com/fsgbooks

To

DENNIS AND DEBORAH CONTA

and in memory of

FABRIZIO MONDADORI

CONTENTS

I

What Was Poetry?

Must We Say What We Mean?

The Wonder of Having Lived Here a Long Time

"Elmer Gantry Was Drunk."

Murray Gell-Mann

Daddy

"Layla"

Epithalamion

II

III

WHAT WAS POETRY?

I hate Christmas, but I hate people
who hate Christmas even more.

JAMES SCHUYLER

No one really knew, though everyone knew what it *should* be;
And now it's just a way of being famous on a small scale.
It was supposed to be significant for its own sake,
Though that was never entirely true: human feelings
Got in the way, for while it was possible to remain unmoved
In the face of all that language, no one really wanted to:
They wanted to talk about it, to explain what it had let them see,
As though the world were incomplete before poetry filled it in.
And now there's nothing left to see: oh, poems come and go
And everyone complains about them, but where there used to be
Arguments there's just appreciation and indifference,
Measured praise that's followed by forgetting. I'm as bad
As anyone: instead of reading I reread, instead of seeing
I remember, and instead of letting silence have its say
I fill it up with talk, as if the last word might be anything else.

And yet despite all this it matters. Sometimes in the midst
Of this long preparation for death that initial solitude returns
And the world seems actual and alive, as it assumes its opposite.

I think the truest thoughts are always second thoughts,
But who am I kidding, other than myself? I hope there's
Someone, that it casts its spell beyond the small cone of light
Hovering over my desk, and that what started out one night
So long ago in silence doesn't end that way. I fantasize
I can hear it somewhere in the realm of possibility,
But only now and then, in intervals between breaths.

MUST WE SAY WHAT WE MEAN?

We're pregnant with it, yet all we can do
Is breathe and wring our hands and shake our heads.
It feels so real, standing for us like the flowers
And the other feelings, which you can't quite see—
Not here or there or anywhere—because it's just yourself,
Complete within itself and inarticulate.
I ran into Fabrizio today, a cruel, chilly April day.
We talked about Eliot and traded Larkin lines
Like *Life is first boredom, then fear.*
Whether or not we use it, it goes,
And leaves what something hidden from us chose,
And age, and then the only end of age. And then
The hardness and the brightness and the plain
Far-reaching singleness of that wide stare//
Is a reminder of the strength and pain
Of being young; that it can't come again,
But is for others undiminished somewhere.

It was an ordinary day upon an ordinary street
Beside a redbrick hall where Emily Hale once taught.
And yet they filled that ordinary atmosphere with feelings
From another century, that felt as momentarily real
As my own, that for a moment *were* my own. It's easy to forget

How miraculous this is—*How . . . how "unlikely"*—
For their nature is to flicker and fade, leaving nothing to say
On their behalf but that they're everything. They're all we have
As long as they last, and all it means to live forever
Is for them to come to life again—as of course they can't,
But for the minor miracle of art. I know that that sounds corny,
But so what? A lot of things sound corny that are true.
Poems are fleeting as the lives they mean, though now and then
They free themselves from time and bring a life to life.
I don't have a clue to how that happens (is it what they *say*?),
How long it lasts or if it even matters, what with poems and lives enough
    enough
To go around—so many people with their feelings, all these poems
That mean, despite their infinite variety, what all poems mean.

THE WONDER OF HAVING

LIVED HERE A LONG TIME

Whatever happened to joke shops? I remember two of them
In downtown San Diego, one on a corner on Broadway
Not far from the library, that specialized in off-color signs,
Like a guy sheepishly imploring "We don't swim in your toilet,
Please don't pee in our pool," or a tall Texan proclaiming
"The high balls are on me." The other was on F Street,
Next door to the Hollywood Burlesque's marquee celebrating
Tempest Storm, with a sign in its window offering fifteen dollars
For 1945 pennies, which I started looking for until it hit me
1945 meant 1,945. Anyway, they're both gone now,

While here I am, inhabiting a moment that supposedly was buried
In those moments I spent looking through their windows sixty years
    ago,
Although I don't believe it. I'm supposed to be a part of nature too,
As subject to its principles as particles and stars. I know time isn't real
And everything that happens happened thirteen billion years ago,
When all of this somehow "occurred." I realize these things,
And yet deep down I think they can't be true: I wasn't even real then
And in a while I won't be real anymore, like the joke shops and
    Tempest Storm

As things turn into time and disappear (though she's still here). And while

That might be just the way things *seem*, it's the way they seem to *me*.

"It feels like such a miracle, this life"—I wrote that in a poem

Six years ago and I repeat it now. I've no idea what other people feel

As they get old, but I feel nothing but amazement, not at *what* I am,

Which is commonplace and ordinary, but *that* I am and have a life at all,

The private one of these appearances beyond the reach of physics.

Though they take the form of time, they're really nothing but myself,

The pages of a narrative that led the way from childhood to here

That no one gets to read unless they want to, pausing to look in the window

Of the joke shop on Broadway on the way to the library, or the one on F Street

Next door to the Hollywood Burlesque. Not to mention Tempest Storm.

"ELMER GANTRY WAS DRUNK."

I saw *Elmer Gantry* in 1960, and was so bowled over by it
I had to read the book. It drew me down the path of modern fiction
That counterbalanced all the math and physics, and though Sinclair
    Lewis
Isn't what he used to be, he led the way to Faulkner and Fitzgerald,
Hemingway, Woolf, Dostoevsky, Joyce, and all those sentences,
Beginning with the first one in the book: "Elmer Gantry was drunk."
For despite the fragmentation and uncertainty, the temporal
    dislocations
And excursions into consciousness, what modernism meant to me
Was language, and the way a sentence could take a transitory
Moment and then make it real. Poetry would come later, but for me
The soul of poetry would always be that underlying prose.

It stayed with me while everything started turning:
High school into college, physics to philosophy, marriage
And Milwaukee, fatherhood, divorce, the years of settled solitude
And the second happiness of marriage, all turning into poetry,
For that's what life becomes if you can get it into words.
I saw *Elmer Gantry* again this afternoon, at Film Forum in New York,
And after almost sixty years and all those books it still holds up.
Burt Lancaster—hated, he claims, by Harvardism, Yaleism, and
    Princetonism—

Still celebrates the majesty of love, "the morning and the evening
    star,"
Until he runs afoul of Lulu Bains, falls temporarily from grace,
And Sister Sharon Falconer, the word of God incarnate, goes up in
    flames.

I had dinner afterwards with Willard Spiegelman at Gene's.
We talked poetry of course, from Howard Moss (who ate there too)
To Amy Clampitt, and I explained my old, unlikely debt to Sinclair
    Lewis,
Which I sensed he wasn't buying, though this poem is witness to it.
And tonight (see how it goes from tense to tense and day to day)
I'm having drinks again at Gene's and dinner with Doug Crase.
We talked about how poetry goes from being something that you
    read
That other people wrote, to being part of what you really are.
For me it was the sense that poems are a way to understand the
    world
As real as math and physics, and as true—something I still believe
That now seems quaint—a sense that came to me from books.

And now I'm back. Going to New York can feel like rereading,
Sometimes even literally—as when Elevator Repair Service reread
    Gatsby
And recounted Benjy's tale. It makes the world feel possible again,
The way it did before I settled into it and made it second nature.
It makes me feel that literature and life both share a sense of destiny,

Floating down a stream of consciousness made up of words so
    mixed up
With the world there isn't any difference. I realize these are fantasies,
Not fairy tales of once upon a time, but narratives that sound like
    real life
And take me back to where I started—borne back ceaselessly
Into a past of perfect sentences, where Caddie smelled like leaves,
Ben's hoarse agony roared about them, Robert Cohn was once
    middleweight
Boxing champion of Princeton, and Elmer Gantry was drunk.

MURRAY GELL-MANN

He was my idol when I was seventeen
And keen on physics. I had breakfast with him
At a math contest in 1963, in a hotel on Mission Bay
In San Diego. I was too starstruck to remember
What we talked about, but I remember his seersucker jacket
And how young he seemed. I wanted to be like him,
Think like him, know what he knew, discover
What he hadn't discovered yet, and now look at me:
Reading his obituary in the *Times* today
I wondered where that life that used to seem so
Clear to me had gone, sitting here in our dining room
In Milwaukee (which to me in 1963 was just a baseball team
Somewhere in the middle of the country), a minor poet
Light-years away from physics, inhabiting his poem.

He saw the patterns in the chaos of cascading particles
Floating in from nowhere like the quarks in *Finnegans Wake*
To fill the openings in some Lie group that he dubbed the Eightfold
    Way,
That had no reason to exist beyond those slots—yet there they were,
As if those patterns were what made them real. What *does* make
    anything real?

I used to think I knew and now I don't. It isn't us, though we're the ones
Who can't stop talking about it since we don't know what it is. I used to think
That physics knew, yet now it makes no sense, not for the usual reasons—
It's strange, shut up and calculate—but since it can't be true
Unless there's nothing there. I could go on, but let me leave it there at
Breakfast with Murray Gell-Mann on Mission Bay in 1963.
Nothing ever came of it, though I remember writing to the president
Of MIT to ask if I should go there first and then Caltech,
Or vice versa. He wrote back to say that either way was fine.

Some things are hidden from us, not because we don't know what they are,
But because they're inconceivable until they happen, like the future.
The morning light in our dining room has the inevitability
Of the ordinary, and yet fifty-seven years ago it was as unreal
As I was then, as unimaginable as that life I had is now.
Sometimes I think the past is all there is. Sometimes I think
It's the other way around, that only now is real. The future though
Remains an abstraction, even when we know what's going to happen, like death,
Especially death. There was supposed to be a different person in this chair.

Where did he go? That universal destination, nowhere? It isn't a
     real question,
Though it sounds like one. It's merely a feeling of perplexity
And calm at the memory I had this morning of someone
I had been and someone I was going to become as I was reading
Murray Gell-Mann's obituary here in our dining room in Milwaukee.

DADDY

Don't worry; it's not what you might think ("Daddy").
It's what we called him all his life, probably a preference
Left over from his Texas upbringing. It was a remarkable life—
Small town Henrietta, deb parties in Dallas, then Columbia
And Juilliard, orchestras in Europe and New York, a Navy NCO
Who hated officers, and then a father figure to the gay
Interior decorators of San Diego, until he died in the saddle
On his way to decorate one last room, where he was going to move.
Yet what I find remarkable today isn't the life itself, but what it
Might have meant to him when he was old, before he died at
    ninety-two.
He'd call his sister every week and got the Henrietta newspaper,
But otherwise it might have never happened: he'd get up early,
    shower,
Read the paper and go back to bed; the rest of the day was waiting
For nothing to occur, sitting in his decorated house amid the
    catalogues
And bric-a-brac, dressed in shorts and leather shoes and knee-length
    socks.
A person's life is everything to him, and while I imagine his was too
I never had a sense of what it meant to him at all: neither pride
Nor disappointment nor regret, or just the fact of all that time
That makes you what you are. The obsession I have with my own

Is overwhelming, though it's not important to anyone but me.
But his didn't seem to matter to him, though it did to me.

Perhaps because the banalities that constitute my life
Wind up in poems, they magnify its meaning; and since his life
Was left unformulated, it felt small. But it's the other way around:
Their objective insignificance makes them raw materials for art
Rather than hagiography; and as for rescuing life from time a poem
Is transitory too, and gone before the life it represents is over.
I'm at the Bean House, where some photographs Tom took of
    Henrietta
Hang on the bedroom wall. There's almost nothing in them: a B&B,
A building that was once a courthouse, and some trees and cars.
Deer walk by as I sit sipping a martini on the deck and looking at the
    sky.
A life is just the sum of its details, but for a while it's all there is,
Until it's over and there's nothing there. It keeps promising
    happiness,
Or at least relief from care, and yet its promises don't matter,
Not because it doesn't keep them, but because happiness and care
Don't matter in the end. I keep thinking of a picture of him in a chair
In the living room, wearing a navy-blue suit and holding his favorite
    cane
While looking at the camera with a bland, accommodating smile.

Physics tells us information can't be lost, and that the time
Of our experience can't be real. So much the worse for physics

You might say—common sense prevails, and nothing can be more real
Than an individual life as it unfolds through time. And yet our lives
Aren't information, but appearances of information, and while
    appearances
Seem real enough, they aren't the world. I don't expect you to agree,
But I don't care. It's simply a way I have of thinking of myself, and
    anyway,
Poems aren't meant to persuade, but just ring true. Maybe it was the
    nervous breakdown
He had in 1962 that made him seem so distant from himself, the
    opposite reaction
Of Saint Sylvia's, whose life seemed even more intense in retrospect
    than it had been
While she was still alive. I don't want to belong, as Leibniz said of
    Berkeley,
"To the class of men who want to be known for their paradoxes," yet
    parts of life
Seem inconsistent with the rest, although we muddle through.
    Mother died
When he was eighty-two and came into his own, no longer bothered
    by the presence
Of the past, as though it hadn't happened, like the way life disappears
    in death—
Not in the obvious sense that it's finally over, but as though the
    conscious part of it
Hadn't been real at all. Most of us spend our lives inside ourselves,
    with only

Now and then an inkling of how tenuous they really are. What did
    persist
For a while wasn't his own world but the one that lay behind it over
    a century ago—
The railroad tracks not far from the house that he grew up in, the
    wooden water tower
Standing next to them, the pecan trees in the backyard hiding
    behind that smile.

"LAYLA"

I never cared for Cream or Eric Clapton's songs,
Though his guitar can break my heart, as it does on "Layla,"
Only not because of the song. Susan and I went to the wedding
Of a friend whose name I can't remember, and her fiancé

Butchie, in a picture-perfect church I still remember on Cape Cod.
There were pews and vows, tuxedoes and a wedding gown
As they came skipping down the church steps, beaming, with a
     bouquet
Held aloft and "Layla" chiming like a hymn of celebration in the
     background,

Prefiguring a happiness that wasn't going to happen, as a truck crash
Left Butchie paralyzed, while she, "She went to the bad." (E.B.)
I barely knew them beyond my memory of their song, but that's
     enough for me.
It's funny how these chance associations that originate so privately

Come to color your world, as though its underlying nature were
     coincidence.
It's funny how what actually occurs—like the wedding and the
     reception

I probably complained about in that annoying way I have—
Becomes irrelevant, while what lodges in your mind years afterwards

Is a shade of feeling that you never even noticed at the time.
When Diane and I get married next year (which no one knows
    about)
There won't be rice or bouquets or white at sixty and seventy-three
Respectively, but after nearly twenty years of it there'll be more

Happiness to come, or so I hope (no truck). It all comes down
To love and luck and a satisfactory playlist we've got to work on
    soon.
"Good Timin'" and "Archie, Marry Me" (as sung by Betty)
Are among the possibilities I suppose. But I don't want "Layla."

EPITHALAMION

I don't know how we did it, but we did.
Weddings may be wonderful in the abstract,
But in reality they're as fraught with peril
As things involving other people always are—
Demands and expectations, unfulfilled
Fantasies and emotions you're supposed to feel
And don't—yet none of that materialized.
Judge Mosley tied our hands with knots, we read our vows,
We went to dinner at a place even my foodie sister loved.
The threatened thunderstorms were no-shows and the evening
Light was lovely on the balcony and in the foyer.
People came from all across the land to let me tell them
You're the only person I know who's truly good.

One of my weaknesses is a temporary certainty
Tempered by second thoughts, and yet I meant it.
No one can live up to what we want or wish we knew,
And yet sometimes I think that wonderful ideal
Of happiness for everyone is yours alone, however vexed
True happiness might be: the uneasy truce between our two cats;
Your perpetually lost glasses; the twilight years of sex.
It's nothing you can step away from and see whole,
Because it's all-consuming and because it's all we have.

Sometimes it doesn't feel like happiness at all, but simply life
At its most immediate and complicated, or the world
Reminding us to grasp it while it's still there,
Still incomplete and vulnerable. I know it's not the
Happiness of the first imagination, but it's what we share.

LIVES

We have them, and live and think about them,
But then, what *are* they? Some seem like
Bigger deals than the rest, like those of big enchiladas
Or the CEOs of banks too big to fail, but why? Some seem
Meaningful for their commitments and accomplishments,
As no doubt they are, though most are unexceptional
And ordinary, and just fine for that. They're all equal
In value, but what that means is difficult to say:
That each one matters more than anything
To whoever's life it is, though each is barely real
To anyone else? The world exists before and after it,
Yet while it breathes it *is* the world, *its* world.
Whenever I attempt to gesture at it, all I find are words
For where I am: this room, this place I live. Stay with me
I want to say, yet it can't, not because it's unreal,
But because I am. Is what I want to say instead
That everything comes down to lives? The thought
Is true enough, but it's a way of feeling, not explaining,
Of poetry rather than a paper. They're real enough I guess,
Just "metaphysically thin." But each of them is everything.

CAPTIVITY

The light dove, cleaving the air in her free flight . . .

KANT

It's about feeling free within the limits,
Without knowing what the limits are.
It's the way I feel each day, and you do too—
Something I mean to talk to you about,
But that meanders off before I can.
It's what it's like to live in an illusion
That continues forever, knowing all the while
That it's ordinary, insignificant and real—
Like Matt Bevis on his mother's complaint
About his captive canaries in the cellar:
"But they're in cages, Matthew." "Yes,"
I said, "but they've got lots of room."

I remember Rogers Albritton sitting in Riegelmann's
In 1985, writing about the will as necessarily free,
And how that means there's no such thing. He dropped that
In the final version, but I still think it's true:
There's all the room in the world for everything
That's actually *in* the world, but what isn't in the world
Are these "free bloody birds" we think we are,

Telling stories to ourselves and pretending that they're true.
The truth lies underneath them, where it can't be seen
And doesn't matter. I like to think that what I can't remember
Isn't real, which is a way of living in the present, or forever.
My life feels continuous, with no sense of limitation
Or an ending, which is its whole point in a way:
There's no one like me it says to no one in particular,
As though it were almost real, and went on forever.

THE REALITY OF THE INDIVIDUAL LIFE

As one who thinks of poetry
As a way of talking to yourself,
I probably do too much explaining,
But that's what talking to yourself is like:
The things you can't explain to anyone
Are suddenly made clear to no one, as though
Nobody mattered but yourself. And it's the same
For each of us, whether you're listening to me or not:
An enveloping cloud of not-quite-language
Hovering on the verge of sense that puts you
At the center of a world that doesn't quite get you,
But of which you're part, a world in which
Each individual life is so completely ordinary
And at the same time so extraordinary it never ends
Until it does: each individual life eternity
In miniature; each life a world.

Yet here I am, lying on my bed
In the middle of the day, feeling the years
Tick by with nothing much to say about them,
As though I'm supposed to. That's the point though,
Isn't it? Without the sense of an individual self
Creating time and bounded by it, I wouldn't be real,

I wouldn't matter, nor would you, despite our
Sentiments and appetites and dreams. It's how we
Differ from our animals, however much we love them—
Something you and I know, but Daisy, sleeping
At the foot of my bed, can't know. Dream on, Daisy.

A ROMANTIC POEM

It's supposed to be solemn and settled
And in celebration of the individual human life,
Whatever it is. It's each of us of course,
And yet the view we have of it is so oblique
It might as well be one of nobody at all,
Or of a vague interior with a figure in a room
Who could be anyone. This sense that it's so close
It must be you: what do we really know of it,
And how could anything that simple be that real?
We would be kings of our domains, alone in majesty
"Above this Frame of things," but those are idle thoughts,
As idle as the vacant pleasures of a summer afternoon.
The truth is much more down to earth: we make things up
And celebrate dejection when we see they can't be real.
Instead of clarity, self-knowledge is a study in confusion,
Driven by the need to see what isn't there. Begun
In gladness, something carries you away until you're
Everyone and no one, for no matter where you are
Or what your name is, it's the same styles
Of thought, the same habits of contemplation
That carry you along to the inevitable conclusion
That life is either ludicrous or not worth living

Or both. But why does it have to be worth anything?
It's just there, the way we're all just there, moving
And needing to be moved, without knowing why.

THE DOGS OF MEXICO CITY

We went before the virus shut things down.
I was expecting a Tijuana of some twenty million,
With car upholstery joints and grilled chicken palaces,
And for a while around the airport so it was.
And then it turned into an almost European city,
With discreet, elegant houses and boulevards and trees,
Probably because Europe kept invading it. I didn't know
It was surrounded by a lake for hundreds of years,
Or that the Aztec temple and the temples it was built upon
Were demolished to make room for the great cathedral
A few hundred yards away, which continues to sink.
Ignacio, our Context tour guide, walked us through its
History, winding up at Diego Rivera's mural
Dream of a Sunday Afternoon in Alameda Park,
That began with Cortez on the left and ended on the right
By Alameda Park, after the lake had disappeared.
We asked Ignacio if he knew Neil Young's great song
"Cortez the Killer," but he said he hadn't heard it.

The anthropological museum goes further back,
With baskets and pottery and figures that resemble dogs
And other small animals, and civilizations with their discontents.
They played a ball game that resembled soccer, but if the ball's
Trajectory deviated from the sun's, "a decapitation was performed,

And the blood would irrigate the soil." Maybe that's why,
Though the Mexica were so much more advanced than anyone
    else
In North America, they couldn't last, for gods stifle all,
And while they had astronomy, Europe had its guns and steel.
It's not enough to live in isolation and in harmony with
Nature and yourself, either as an individual or a whole civilization—
There are always Others. Yet I'm not writing this to moralize
Or explain. I'm writing this to celebrate the dogs of Mexico City,
Who were everywhere, in all shapes and sizes, mostly small.

When I was a kid, there was usually an ad in comic books
With a Chihuahua in a teacup pleading, "Please give me a home."
My best friend Kenny (Carlos) had a friendly dog named Lanni,
Whose puppy Mitzi my parents finally let me bring home.
Maybe that's why I think of dogs and Mexico together,
Or maybe dogs and Mexico just enjoy each other's company.
In any case, those dogs were everywhere, deliriously happy
In the parks and on their leashes, with Diane distraught
Because she didn't know enough Spanish to ask to pet them.
We never saw a single cat (or a single Subaru for that matter),
And they never barked, but were part of the surroundings,
Like the taxis and the trees. It's wonderful to be somewhere else
And still yourself: history disappears, and everything comes down
    to you,
The two of you, walking through the parks and streets, me
    complaining
About my feet and Diane hailing Uber. By the time we got home

The virus was set to start, and Mexico City slipped back into
    memory
And history, with its monuments and museums, its European
    boulevards
And parks, the vanished Lake Texcoco that once surrounded it,
    the delirious
Dogs in their habitat that never barked, and not a single cat.

SHELTERING AT HOME

But sometimes standing still is also life.

JOHN ASHBERY

I hate it—but then home
Was always a place to depart from
Or come back to, not a state of being in itself.
In the morning it's my face in the mirror
And the newspaper in an easy chair, but then
I'm back on the shelf for the rest of the day,
While outside the weather has its way
And it's not good. Now and then I go for a drive
To prove the existence of an external world
Of houses and trees and no people, but most of the time
I stay in my room, while Diane works in her study.
The nostalgia for the ordinary, for the world
Of just a month or so ago keeps overwhelming me,
Although my life then was the same as it is now.
We live in our imaginations, and if the world
Isn't up to them our lives aren't either: instead of
Lofting us "above this Frame of things,"
They sink back into it, yet continue somehow.

"Over 2,000 Illustrations and a Complete Concordance"
Is a kind of travelogue that culminates in a childhood

Far away from home, in a way of remaining alone
Without knowing it, of not knowing where or what you are.
Driving in my car to Wingspread or Port Washington,
I realize I'm going there instead of staying home
Because I want to, but also because without a destination
Life feels like nowhere, like a story without an ending
Or a vast metropolis that takes you in and leaves you on your own.
I know it's moods and cabin fever, but what is there to go on
But a sense of purpose, however small? What is it but a travelogue,
Even when you're inside—especially when you're inside,
Where you think you're free to roam because there's no place else
     to go?
Let's face it—you can't. We like to think of the imagination
As inexhaustible and transcendent, but it's as earthbound as we are
As we cling to an idea of someplace better than the one we have.
You believe you see it through the window, but it's just your own
Reflection in the mirror, in the morning when the world
Feels simultaneously too close and too far away. It isn't home
Or even close to home, and yet it's where and what you are.

ON BEING DEAD

Well, not quite, though Diane keeps calling me
Her horizontal husband, since after I finish the paper
And my laptop rounds, I just lie down on the bed
And close my eyes and contemplate the vacuum of the day.
The Great Outdoors is a place in my head, too far away
To visit, and instead of something to look forward to,
The future is a butter burger from a drive-through, a solitary
Session on the balcony and eventually the cocktail hour.
I'm happy that I'm sheltered by the flowers and the trees,
As in that cemetery I hope is still a little ways away,
But really, what's the point if all there is to life
Is whatever gets you through the day? It's over the top,
This poem, but I don't care. What I care about is something—
Anything—to alleviate the monotony and isolation of our lives
This sheltering makes explicit. Do I really believe that?
It's so hard to say, since a mood swamps everything,
And what you feel today is an embarrassment tomorrow.
I only know I'm living in the interval between
The luxuries of consciousness and the straits of sorrow,
A bare condition of mere being in which nothing changes
And a life is just the sum of its details as it slowly slips away.

GOING ON

I keep repeating myself in alternative ways,
Which is how I get through the days—
Quietly pretending that there's nothing else in store
And *now* is the mirror of *was*,
While living with the sense that there must be *something more*,
Although I don't know what it is;
Quietly living behind the veil of appearance
With a fragile sense of clearance.

AMNESIA FOR THE FUTURE

I don't remember what it was supposed to be like,
Except that it was going to be open. There weren't any details,
Beyond the ones so clichéd they carried you along through
Everyday daydreams—a new car or turntable, travel, accolades—
But that was part of the fun, the fun of something new.
And now it's the same thing every day, the same imagination,
The same imagery. I can't even talk about what's happening now,
Although I'd like to, because nothing's going to happen next.
I'd like to sum things up, and yet there's no totality without a future
To contain it, and no future without those individual lives that make
    it up.
They used to be like diaries or minor novels, histories of themselves
That wrote their stories as they went along, then told them to
    themselves:
Alone, yet always on the way to somewhere else, an unfamiliar place
Where others made up stories of their own that were essentially the
    same.
There's no place left to go now, no vantage point a life in progress
Might aspire to, to try to rest and understand itself, and then try to
    explain.
There's only life at home, where every future is the same one you
Wake up to, and experience and its explanation are the same.

—

My world is a receding world. I suppose it's coming back
Eventually, but whether there'll be time enough to bridge the gulf
Between a life and everything it promises is anybody's guess.
What Wordsworth called "the wonder of disappointment"
Is a kind of consolation that the future offers while those promises
Abide unkept, as though the fact of their existence were enough.
I don't want to make too much of it, but as the days succeed each
    other
Without comment and their monotone becomes a style of going on,
I keep feeling that in lieu of a conclusion none of this is ever going
    to end,
With the same perplexities and explanations repeating themselves
Over and over again, on an exponentially diminishing scale.
I wouldn't even mind it if I understood it or could see the point:
A permanent condition of existence to supplant the old one
Based on progress, or a way of living in the details of each day?
I even like the way the morning starts with reading, which continues
Through the afternoon, and evening ends with my appointment
    with a record.
But those are merely ways of going along with something I don't get,
Whose underlying rationale, assuming it even has one, remains
    opaque.

I wonder if the life I used to have was really all that different.
I like to think it focused on the future, putting off the satisfactions
Of the moment for the sake of something better, but who am I
    kidding?

I've always lived from day to day, and if in retrospect a narrative
Emerged it sprang from wishful thinking and forgetting.
It's tempting to believe that anything that happens in the world
Or in a newspaper could change your life, for that's the story from
    inside.
The truth is that we're resolute and small, and all this sensitivity
To circumstance is simply self-importance. What difference does
    it make
If I'm disgruntled with myself? We all have moments when the
    future
Loses its point, but what matters are these constant reassessments
And the semblance of a life they offer, even when that sense of life
    is bleak.
As long as something real still speaks to me my life remains my own,
And even if the burden of its message is a long complaint, it's still
    complete.
I wouldn't call it fun, and yet at least it's something you can
    recognize
When you wake up, and get along with as you navigate the day,
Pausing now and then like this along the way to God knows where—
For even while the future feels so out of reach, it's there.

LIFE IN RHYME

It's faster, and also feels more complete.
Instead of dragging on from day to day
While nothing happens, something like the way
Nothing happens in dreams, you can delete

The boring parts and come right to the point:
I only exist because I say so—
Something I might have said after a joint
I smoked forty or fifty years ago

That turned out to be true, with one stanza
Following another from thence to hence,
A simulacrum of experience
Approaching its ultimate cadenza

With a smile, only to shrug and back off,
Since the boring parts are the real ones.
I want to believe that everything runs
On a predetermined course from liftoff

To touchdown, even though it isn't true.
Consider St. Joseph's, San Diego,
My obsession with Marvin K. Brown's new
Cadillacs, track, trips to the Borrego

Desert and science fairs: they're my story
Now, but they didn't feel like anything
At the time, waiting for the bell to ring
And turn my school days into history.

Young adulthood and early middle age
Felt like that too—like a lot of nothing,
With now and then an arrow or a sling
Of fortune that turned out to be a page

Turning in hindsight, when I didn't care.
Six years ago I wrote a poem about
Coming home and finding there's nothing there.
Getting old means coming to live without

That sense of inevitability
People used to feel when they were young and
Don't anymore. I just don't understand
How they stand that indeterminacy

About the future, which was always there,
Although easy to hide. It's wide open
Now and gets celebrated everywhere,
Only I don't buy it. I'd misspoken

Earlier when I said my existence
Depended on what I said: it doesn't
Depend on anything, since it wasn't
Anything to begin with—just a tense,

Past, present or future. I simply try
To inhabit it, carry my own torch
A while and communicate some of my
Thoughts. I think we should go out on the porch.

WORLDS ENOUGH AND TIME

It's presumptuous, but if you're reading this you
Probably know my usual obsessions and preoccupations:
The "world"—both the word and what it stands for—and time,
Which is or isn't real, depending on my mood. I've always
Hated poems about philosophy, and I hope I still do,
But since I don't know what that means anymore, here I am,
Musing on my ends and my beginnings one more time,
As though to be alive were just to wonder what they were,
While all the while inhabiting three worlds: the private world
That's coextensive with my life and ends with it; the world
That everyone inhabits, that's indifferent to anything that anyone
Believes or feels; and the problematic one behind them both
That spreads through time in ways that make it hard
To understand how the other two could possibly be real.

Meanwhile I'm on the balcony with a drink in my hand
And looking at the leaves. If I were a different kind of poet
I'd note the contrast with a deprecating irony and just leave it there,
But I'm not and I won't. People write books about philosophy and
    physics
We're supposed to understand and don't, and nobody complains.
Life is more complex than either, since it includes them both, yet
    poems,

Which are simply life articulated, are supposed to be as clear as day
To anyone who takes the time to read them on the run. When I'm
    asked
What my poems say, I say that it's whatever's on my mind—for life
Means having something on your mind, whether you understand it
    or not.
Right now it's the idea that as it flows through time the world keeps
Branching into versions of itself, and I do too—an idea that's meant
    to be
Pure mathematics, though I haven't got a clue to what it means.

Whatever else exists beyond the page of the mind, there's
Someplace hidden from us where we don't exist at all. I guess
It's all around us, though by definition we don't really know.
I went to a talk this afternoon on the quaint idea of God
Philosophers of religion love to play around with, though I didn't
Stay for the discussion, since I didn't want to play. I grew up
    believing
Something like it; then it disappeared. Theories have to answer
To both our private and public worlds, and that one didn't.
Sometimes I wonder if the hidden world I do believe in isn't
    doomed
To vanish too, since it can't accommodate the others, as the mind
Of seventy-three can't understand the infant consciousness it used
    to be
And can't even imagine anymore. Confined to the imagination
Or released from it, you're limited to what you understand and feel,

Which keeps diminishing over the years, until you're finally
Left with nothing new to say. I hope they'll get it right someday,
Though by then I'll be gone. For now, feeling it's something
I don't understand will have to do, sitting out here on the balcony
Under the trees and an empty blue sky, looking at the leaves
And living within the limits. And anyway, it's what I want to do.

LATE, LATE SHOW

I never read John O'Hara's stories, but having read them
Now they all seem pretty much alike. There's a lot of
Background and a few remarks before not very much happens
And the story ends, and apparently things are somehow changed.
I never even *thought* of reading them, yet now I like the way
They sometimes sound the way I like to think life feels, full of
Nuances and nothing, in which nothing's ever heightened
Or exaggerated, and something unspoken and unrealized remains.
I even like the way they're disappointing, and the way he's
    disappointed
Too inside those Yale dreams he had in Pottsville, Pennsylvania—
The reciprocal resentments of the stories he embodied and the ones
    he wrote.
They're called *New Yorker* Stories now that no one writes them
    anymore
And no one lives the way they used to live in them, or understands
The code of conduct they implied for everything one did or said or
    wrote,
When almost everything was implied—hanging on something
Somebody suggested in a bedroom in the east eighties, or left unsaid
To someone sitting next to them at a late-night table at the Colony
    or 21.

—

I began by wondering what poetry used to be, and what it's now
    become.
It still means everything to me, though to nearly everyone I know
It doesn't exist anymore, if it ever did. Sometimes I think I'm terrified
That it was all a style, like John O'Hara's or a restaurant's or a way of
    talking
That's had its day, and I've wasted my life. Of course I hasten to say
That I don't believe it for a moment, and that the fact of its near
    invisibility
Is a sign of how much it actually matters. Still, it means that in the
    last analysis
You're all alone, and that the only proof of its importance is your
    own.
What is this craving for validation? When John O'Hara received
    the Gold Medal
From the American Academy of Arts and Letters he stood up and
    wept,
And then retired to Princeton and the life he thought it owed him,
To no avail. Stellification comes too late to make a difference
If it comes at all, because it's always about to happen or because it's
    over
Before anyone even notices. Either way, you can't know whether
It was real or just an exercise in self-delusion, for whichever it
    might be
The view from where you are remains the same, with nothing to
    go on
But the trying, and dying for it to happen again and again.

THE DAY,

as in "back in," which was never really there.
I dislike the myth of the exceptional past,
Since everyone has one, but let's face it: the sixties
Really *were* exceptional, though no one cared at the time,
And they could seem silly (remember bell-bottoms?).
Art, politics and music were aligned for a while,
Not so much in agreement as in clarity, and though
Even poetry seemed part of it, that wasn't true,
Since poetry is never really part of anything,
Though it wants to be. I discovered New York Poets
In 1965, when Lewis brought Peter Schjeldahl
And Kenward Elmslie to campus to read, and afterwards
We went to a bar off Witherspoon Street, where some guys
From my eating club yelled, "Close the door Hairpiece"
At Peter as we stumbled in from the cold.

It's all jumbled now: the poems we read,
The poems we wrote, the poems we talked about
For hours and then forgot. I remember Peter saying
"Clepsydra" is the poem of our time, on the way
To a party at Jane Freilicher's after a reading of John's
In New York, and he was right. "You'll be so great
When you move to New York," Linda told me

When I said something catty, though I never did move—
I just circled around it as though it were the sun, and still do.
I haven't seen Peter in almost twenty years,

And now he's dying in *The New Yorker*.
"Everybody dies," as Stephen Sondheim says
In *Company*, and yet it still seems so unreal.
We're going to see *Company* in New York in April,
But it won't be the same. Peter brought New York back
To me as it probably never was, the way it was to me.
Reading him that life returned, though nothing in particular
Returned, since life isn't particulars but possibilities
And ideas of particulars, more real in the abstract
And in memory than they were when they were just alive.
He said that there's no yellow patch in *View of Delft*,
Yet there are three, though there was only one when Bergotte died.
It made me feel nineteen again, and also on the verge
Of death, as though inhabiting an imaginary state of mind
When poetry and the possibility of poetry, New York
And the idea of New York were both the same, instead of
Disparate and real. But that was back in the day.

OBVIOUS DAYS

FOR MATT BEVIS

We made a happy home and there we pass our obvious days.

EDWARD LEAR

They still have their surprises, but there's nothing they conceal
They're preparing us for: not the new long poem I'm going to write
Eventually, or something we're going to do that's different
From what we couldn't imagine twenty years ago, and then did.
I miss the thrill of the unexpected, but as someone no doubt said, diminished
Expectations are a kind of happiness too, as fit for celebration as the rest.
I know it sounds so second-rate, which is how the present always feels
By contrast with the potential of the past and promise of a future
That shrinks as you get older and turn into what you are. And it's easy,
Too easy. But the more you think about happiness, the more elusive
It becomes. And the more you think about yourself the more unreal you are.

—

I believe both that there's *something else*, and that there isn't—

Keats's "negative capability," the ability to make no sense and
    mean it,

Or Fitzgerald's idea of intelligence as a power to harbor
    contradictory thoughts

And still get by, though all I share with them are sentences and
    confusions.

I used to take more pride in it than I do now, as though it masked
    a truth I knew

That other people didn't, though it's really just a style that seems
    to point beyond itself

And helped me make it through the days when they did too. I love
    our life,

Despite the fact there's nothing that it lacks. I love the way it keeps
    its promises

And promises so little. Most of all I love the equilibrium between its

Highs and lows, its ups and downs—between the lovely morning
    sunlight

And the disappointments limited to the weather and the evening
    news.

I'm in a reading group trying to fathom Heidegger, a philosopher I
    dislike,

Though I'll give anything a try. He seems to think we've lost a grasp

Of what it is to *be* the Greeks once had, and that we need it back.
    He manifests

An overweening sense of struggle I instinctively distrust, that tempts
   me too.
Why can't ordinary happiness be enough, or even everyday
   unhappiness?
There's nowhere else to go, and even if there were it would be just
   another home,
Another life within its limits. People think that heaven could be
   anywhere but here,
Though it can't be, since it isn't anywhere. I know all that. And yet
   I'm moved
By things I know can't possibly be true, since here is always where
   we are—
Like the story of Owl and Pussy-cat sailing away in their little boat
To a land that's merely somewhere in a poem, but where they finally
   find
True happiness on the edge of the sand, by the light of the moon.

THE AFTERLIFE

is some lectures by Samuel Scheffler that aren't about
Heaven or immortality, but a sustained thought experiment
About our imminent demise, either suddenly from some
Foreseeable catastrophe, or less quickly, as we lose the ability
To perpetuate ourselves and gradually die out. It's about the way
The future shapes us, and how things that matter to us now
And what we care about depend on it in ways that it's exasperating
To explain but still feel real. If the point of life were simply to be
    happy
For as long as you're around, why should it make any difference
What happens when you're gone, or if anyone else is there?
And yet it does. We live for possibility and the feeling of the future,
And a life is meaningful by being part of something else that
    carries on.
I write this with mortality hanging in the air, and even though no
    one will read it
In ten or twenty or a hundred years, if I believed that wasn't even
    possible
I don't believe I could. The void I speak into is filled with people
Who could hear me even if they won't, and without that possibility
    of history
The present isn't fully real. History erases us yet makes us what
    we are

While we're alive: I wake up every morning to tomorrow
And the past, but take away their sense of something still to come
And where it came from and I'm sheltering in place, without
A sense of being or a life, a real life. It's a different thought experiment,
This life, but regardless of its outcome the conclusion is the same:
A world of one, existing in proximity to those other worlds
I can't quite imagine, but which make it something everyone can see—
An ordinary person sitting on his balcony on a summer afternoon,
Waiting patiently for someone to explain it to and meanwhile
Living quietly in his imagination, imagining the afterlife.

BEYOND BELIEF

Th'expense of spirit in a waste of shame

Perhaps it *is* like lust, this urge for something
More than what there is. I was brought up Catholic,
With all the superstition that entails. Then we became
Lutheran, which was worse, since it was supposed to be
More literal, which only made it more intense.
And then sometime in high school it all just fell away,
Leaving me with that vague sense of spirituality
You wrestle with in poems, without knowing what it is.
My mother slid into a kind of transcendentalism
Centered on an Emersonian divinity within,
And I guess that I did too, with all these celebrations
And deflations of the self embodied in their disillusionments.
It's a different sort of religion, one without doctrines
Or sacraments, although the danger of delusion is the same,
The temptation of an inarticulate form of knowledge
Gathering in the life that hides behind your name.
And yet I want that knowledge, even if it's specious,
Like an expense of spirit in a waste of shame.

The same songs linger to be sung, and no matter
How demotic, they feel like hymns without the pews.

The same perplexities await relief, relief that
Can't be formulated. The long perspective on yourself
And on the world transcends belief, yet it's a superstition too,
Without being a denomination. Wonder at them both
Should be enough, without making it a question of their nature
Or creation, and yet that seems so difficult to do. I live here
In the space between attention and belief, attempting to believe
That leaving everything as it is might see me through—
As of course it can, though everything seems like a miracle,
Not a miracle to be interrogated, just a miracle. The hard part
Is to find yourself at home with where and what you are
And still remain amazed: the days go by, the morning brings
A feeling of complacency, the sense of wonder dissipates
And begins to feel like second nature, turning into something
You can talk about and even try to understand, an ordinary mystery.
But beneath it lies something you can hold in your hand.

O you I conjure up, to whom I speak as to myself, listen:
These arguments and back-and-forths are what life comes to
When you start to wonder what it is. Instead of insight,
Knowledge and relief from care, it becomes a voice, the voice
Of someone talking to himself that he begins to think of as his own.
I started writing poetry because in reading it I thought I heard myself,
Which made it seem like such an easy thing to do. I didn't
Realize at first that what appears so settled on the page
Is just the face of the continuous confusions of the inner life
It hides, and that no matter how inevitable it sounds it isn't true.

I go on wondering what to say, suspecting all the while
That in the end it doesn't matter, because what else is there to do,
Beyond remaining mute with amazement—which I can't,
Having neither the ability nor the will. I keep saying the same things
Over and over, until they turn into a prayer or an admonishment,
An admonishment that feels like a prayer, like someone else's prayer:
Teach me to care and not to care, teach me when to turn around,
When to speak and when to shut up. Teach me to sit still.

A WAY OF PUTTING IT

1

Unfortunately, I'm given to the pronouncements of age
As I get older, but it isn't complacency or the cocktail hour.
It's simply the frustration of revising what I used to feel
And hope in order to accommodate the demands of the page

Of seventy-four, or to see myself anew through "ancient,
Glittering eyes" while being faithful to what I've been all along,
As it alters slightly in the changing light, while remaining
A version of what it always was, like an echo of the same song.

In the end what matters is the feeling of life as a whole
As reflected in the details of each day, which are difficult to see.
As truth becomes altered in the telling, so the individual life
Becomes an artifact of its history, no matter what its original goal

Might have been, or what it might be happy to settle for now.
And it's not just the individual life, but the collective life of art
That's subject to revision, however unimportant it's become,
Involving at the same time both "a wholly new start,

And a different kind of failure," which feel the same.
Sosostris, Eugenides, Sunday Morning from the Palisades
And Innisfree—what hides behind every "order of monuments"
Is an ordinary person with the usual anxieties and a name

That might be anyone's. That's what I still find so extraordinary
After all these years: that however transcendent the outcome,
What it articulates is there for everyone to see, and whatever else
You might aspire to, anything you ultimately become

Is what everyone becomes. But even though what you feel
Is of no importance sub specie aeternitatis, and isn't even
Conceivable by anyone else, it's the only thing that matters
For the short while it lasts, the only thing that's real.

2

I suppose that most of this is true
In a sense that's important to me alone,
But basically I'm an ordinary person
With a life that's much like your own
Except for the details, whose significance
Resides in its insignificance—somebody
Factual and prone to please, good company,
A "smiling public man." I have my own history
Too, involving California and Catholicism,
Whose demands were so severe that when my
Dear Baptist grandmother Nana died in Texas,
I knew she'd burn in hell forever for her sin.

It felt more human once religion fell away,
To be replaced by microscopes and chemistry,
Then by science fairs and track, mathematics
And physics and a final collapse into decadence,
As smoking, philosophy and poetry had their way.
I dwell so much on the years when I was young
Because they last forever, and they set the tone
For whatever happens later with increasing speed,

Like variations on the themes I'm skipping over:
Marriages, homes, careers, interests I lost interest in
And friends who still matter to me as they disappear,
Leaving nothing but the facts I've summarized.

I feel this ambivalence about the personal,
So let me try to make it clear. It's real enough
As far as it goes, but in the end it's just a disguise
Of a different kind, one that leaves out everything
Of importance that you can't articulate, like the sense
Of what it feels like to be impermanent and alive.
Even though I say one thing and mean another,
Even though "everything I'm telling you may be a lie,"
The underlying poem is a part of the imagination,
Mine or someone else's, and as it reveals itself
Without autobiography, it embodies the sense of a life
That's no one's, and of what it's like for it to be your own.

3

Who cares whose voice it is, as long as it's alive?
I've heard it now for sixty years, and yet I don't know
What it says, or why it sometimes makes me cry.
It isn't my story in particular, or anyone's,
Though it captures the tone of what it's like to think so
For a while, and the way life feels as it goes by.
It all adds up to something in the end, even if it was there
All along and I didn't see it. It doesn't change
Or outlast anything, or reveal anything that isn't clear—
It just touches me this way, and makes me glad.

The deepest happiness is to see the ordinary world
For what it is, but to see it without sadness.
You look at it over and over through your own eyes
And the words of others, but always for the first time.
I sit here on my balcony looking at the same sky
I remember from high school and the poems I loved in college,
And it's as though I'd never seen it before, and the feeling
"Of being absolutely safe" Wittgenstein described were my own.
It's a poem captured from the air in a voice that's undefined,
Which as it starts to deepen and increase feels like mine.

—

The simple soul that issues from the hand of God;
The necklace that's a carving not a kiss; the bee-loud glade
That gathers from the air a live tradition . . . I don't think
They were ever the little world I wanted them to be,
But it meant everything to me to think they were, and still does.
I'm writing this without embarrassment, because no matter
How inconsequential it's become, and how beside the point it seems,
It still defines my life, and occupies it like a waking dream.
It isn't the sudden shaft of sunlight or the gradual transformation
Of experience or the unkept promise of a different life—

It's simply that I'm happy. I like the sense of being
Part of something larger than myself, of telling you about it
As I try to remember how it started, and wondering how much
Longer its presence in my heart is going to last. I'd like to say
Forever, but that's an exercise in futility, and isn't even what I want.
It's sufficient that the past remain the past, this summer afternoon
Be simply what it is, and the future . . . ? I've gone on enough:
Instead of reaching a conclusion, getting older is a study in tone
That leaves you where you are—still listening to yourself
A lifetime away from where you started, and not far from home.

ACKNOWLEDGMENTS

Some of the poems in this book first
appeared in the following publications:

Glimpse: "The Afterlife," "Daddy"

Hampden-Sydney Review: "Life in Rhyme,"
"Must We Say What We Mean?"

Iterant: "'Elmer Gantry Was Drunk.',"
"The Wonder of Having Lived Here a Long Time"

Manchester Review: "Captivity," "Obvious Days"

The New Republic: "'Layla,'" "A Romantic Poem"

The New York Review of Books: "Late, Late Show"

Oxeye Reader: "Going On," "On Being Dead"

The Paris Review: "Lives," "The Reality of the Individual Life"

Poetry: "Murray Gell-Mann"

Raritan: "A Way of Putting It," "Beyond Belief"

The Yale Review: "The Day," "Worlds Enough and Time"

"Sheltering at Home" appeared in the anthology
Together in a Sudden Strangeness (Alfred A. Knopf)

"What Was Poetry?" appeared in *The FSG Poetry
Anthology* (Farrar, Straus and Giroux) and
The Unamuno Author Series Festival Anthology

9 780374 607869